DEPARTED WINGS

The post deregulation decade

Los Angeles International Airport
LAX

1980 -1990

About the photos

Over a decade ago, I came across a box of 35mm airline slides at a local estate sale. That box held wonderful snapshots of the past, frozen in time, of airliners and airports of the West Coast during the decade of the 1980s. Having no real experience in slide collecting, I sought to start a collection and preserve these *"windows"* of the past. Over the past ten years, using a variety of sources, including purchasing private collections, online auctions, and airline memorabilia conventions, I have amassed thousands of slides, mainly with a focus on the 1980s time period. The photos in this book are the result of this specific collection of slides.

First published in 2018 by Departed Wings LLC, PO Box 694 Atwood, California, 92811.

© Jon Jamieson, 2018.

All rights reserved. No part of this book may be reproduced or transmitted in any form or by any means, electronic or mechanical, including photocopying, recording, or by an information storage and retrieval system - except by a reviewer who may quote brief passages in a review to be printed in a magazine or newspaper - without permission in writing from the publisher.

ISBN 978-1-7322600-0-9

Book printed in China

Visit us at: www.departedwings.com
or on Facebook at: www.facebook.com/DepartedWings

Front Cover: A classic scene at LAX during the early 1980s; the famous theme building along with a Pacific Southwest Airlines (PSA) McDonnell Douglas MD-81 taxiing away from the terminal complex.

Back Cover: A Trans World Airlines (TWA) Lockheed L-1011 on final approach to Runway 24 Right during a early winter rainstorm in December 1985.

Introduction

The decade of the 1980s can arguably be considered one of the most exciting and interesting periods in the annals of commercial aviation. On the heels of the Airline Deregulation Act of 1978, hundreds of new airlines, both large and small, were started to fill the void left by the legacy carriers. These new airlines were established for many reasons including, catering specifically to business class passengers, focusing on vacation destination points or connecting small, local communities that had seen airline service cease after the deregulation legislation. Most of these start-up airlines failed, some lasting only a few months, save a few, which weathered the *"storm,"* and prospered though the 1980s and into the decade of the 1990s. The 1980s, were a decade of transition, as the introduction of new quieter, fuel-efficient, longer range aircraft, such as the Boeing 757, Boeing 767, and McDonnell Douglas MD-80 would be operated alongside the *"classics,"* including the Douglas DC-8 and Boeing 707. The common airliners of the time, such as the Boeing 727, 737, 747, Douglas DC-10, and Lockheed L-1011, continued to be frequent tenants at the airports, popular on both domestic and international services. Flying was no longer constrained to the rich and famous, and millions of passengers experienced flying first hand on trips of both business and pleasure. As the 1980s waned, a series of mergers resulted in the larger legacy airlines purchasing the smaller, regional carriers that once pioneered air-routes within their own geographic regions. Airlines such as Western, AirCal, Ozark, Republic, and Frontier were quickly absorbed into the operations of their new parent airlines, while their trademark service and logos were lost to the history books. Los Angeles became the nucleus of airline traffic in the popular Southern California market, as local, regional, national, and international airlines vied for coveted gate space at the growing airport. As one of the largest and busiest airports in the world during the 1980s, Los Angeles International Airport (LAX) held a significant awe, for the occasional traveler, seasoned passenger, and airline enthusiast alike. This book is not meant as a total catalog of all the airlines or aircraft that transited the Los Angeles International Airport during the 1980s, but rather to provide a look back at a truly great time in the evolution and growth of the global, commercial airline industry.

LAX   LOS ANGELES INTERNATIONAL AIRPORT

At the start of the commercial aviation age, Los Angeles was in transition from a small, sleepy, hacienda village to a bustling metropolis. The city once surrounded by citrus groves and cattle ranches was being transformed into houses, streets, and commercial centers. In the early years of aviation, many small airports operated in the region with passenger services flying from the "main" airport located in Burbank (Union Air Terminal), just north of the city. In 1928, the City of Los Angeles purchased a large plot of agricultural land, west of the city, near the communities of El Segundo and Inglewood and just a few miles east of the Pacific Ocean. Christened, *"Mines Field,"* a large parking lot, hangers, and three dirt runways were constructed in time for the National Air Races held in September of 1928. The new airport hosted numerous air race expositions, flight schools and the aura of early aviation well into the 1930s, yet passenger services continued to be flown from neighboring Burbank airport. After World War II, Los Angeles saw the growing need for a modern airport facility and developed a master plan that would realign the field to better accommodate passenger and freight aircraft. In 1946, a new terminal, office buildings and asphalt runways were constructed, and later that year four out of the five airlines (United, American, Trans World and Western) serving the existing Burbank Airport relocated to the new Los Angeles Airport. As passenger demand for air travel grew in the post-war years, Los Angeles slowly expanded to serve the existing carriers and accommodate new airlines and aircraft. Twin-engine Douglas DC-3 and Convair 240s were replaced with the four-engine Douglas DC-4s and eventually the longer range and luxurious, Lockheed Super Constellation and Douglas DC-7C *"Seven Seas"* aircraft. The new, longer range aircraft, permitted non-stop routings from Los Angeles, to cities such as Chicago, Dallas and New York, which made travel quicker and more efficient. In 1954, Scandinavian Airline System (SAS), made history by starting flights into Los Angeles via an *"over-the-pole,"* multi-stop route using a Douglas DC-6B, and provided the airport with its first, direct international route to Europe. As the Los Angeles metropolitan region continued to grow at a tremendous rate, the availability and popularity of air travel increased in step. During the late 1950s, a major program to expand the airport for anticipated growth and jet traffic was started. This ambitious project, with construction starting in 1957, included extending and expanding the existing two runways, adding modern aircraft terminals, vehicle parking structures, a new control tower and a centralized *"theme"* building. History was made in January 1959, when American Airlines inaugurated the first jet service to the airport, with non-stop flights to New York City, using its brand new Boeing 707-123. The year 1959, also brought two new international airlines to Los Angeles; both REAL Brasil (later VARIG) and Japan Airlines started flights to the airport and further solidified the status of the region. Construction of the new airport facilities was completed by 1963, and the *"Jet Age,"* was in full swing, as older piston powered aircraft made way for the sleek transports that made flying more affordable and convenient. Throughout the 1960s, LAX grew to serve over twenty-two different airlines, twelve of them being international carriers, and was recording over one hundred arrivals and departures daily. By the 1970s, LAX had become a global presence in the world annals of commercial aviation. New, *"Jumbo Jet,"* Boeing 747s, and wide-body Lockheed L-1011 and Douglas DC-10 aircraft, brought thousands of passengers from over five continents, non-stop, into Los Angeles. The list of both domestic and international airlines grew to serve the megalopolis of sunny Los Angeles, which had grown to become home to over four million people. During the early decade of the 1980s, another major expansion project was underway to bring LAX further into the future of modern aviation and provide an exemplary airport for both business and pleasure travelers, whether local or from afar.

From January 1, 1980, through December 31, 1990, Los Angeles International Airport (LAX) was served by over one hundred twenty (120) different airlines, flying over thirty types of aircraft, with flights extending out to five different continents. Some airlines lasted throughout the entire decade, while others survived for only a few months. These following pages hold a glimpse of the past, a time when color defined an airlines identity and aircraft represented innovative progress. Look back on one of the most fascinating and colorful periods of commercial aviation and let your mind drift back to a time of deafening takeoff noise, the strong smell of jet exhaust and the splendor of vibrant color schemes. Sit back and enjoy these departed wings………

Of the eighty-four airlines that are pictured in this book, only twenty-seven remain in service at the end of 2017. All images in this book were taken at LAX on the dates given.

January 1980

Continental Airlines first started operations into Los Angeles in 1957, with *"Gold Carpet"* service flights from Denver, using the Douglas DC-7B. Only six years later, in 1963, would the airline move its headquarters to Los Angeles and form an extensive route system from the airport. In 1969, the airline started service from Los Angeles to Honolulu, using Boeing 707s and established the airline's Hawaiian and Micronesian strong-hold for which it became well-known. The airline received its first of eight, originally ordered, Douglas DC-10-10s in 1972, and inaugurated service with the 345-passenger wide-body, on its popular Los Angeles-Denver-Chicago route. By 1980, Continental was serving twelve cities from Los Angeles, and was using its *"Heavy 10s"* on flights to Chicago, Denver, Honolulu, and Houston. Preparing to take Runway 24 Left for a morning departure is N60854, a Douglas DC-10-10CF, one of the few convertible passenger/freighter options for which Continental Airlines was the launch customer.

March 1981

Evergreen International Airlines was originally formed in 1960, as a helicopter charter company based in McMinnville, Oregon. During 1975, the helicopter charter was merged with an aircraft charter business and Evergreen International Airlines was formed. With the passage of cargo airline deregulation in 1977, Evergreen entered the cargo business by flying contract charters from New York City in 1980. Evergreen acquired an overnight freight contract with United Parcel Service (UPS) in 1981, and Douglas DC-9 aircraft were purchased for this service. Cargo services were operated along the West Coast and daily flights covered a Los Angeles-San Francisco-Portland-Seattle route, as well as a non-stop Los Angeles-Seattle service, using a mix of Douglas DC-9 and Lockheed L-188 Electra aircraft. Evergreen International Airlines continued to provide both contract cargo and passenger services from Los Angeles throughout the 1980s. Parked at the northern cargo ramp is N932F, a Douglas DC-9-32F.

March 1981
The famous flag carrier of the United Kingdom, British Airways, was the result of the merger between British Overseas Airways Corporation (BOAC) and British European Airways (BEA) in 1972. BOAC had modest beginnings in 1939, when Imperial Airways was taken over and flights to overseas destinations such as Africa and India continued. In 1946, the airline was given authority to fly to both North America and the Far East, and Boeing *"Stratocruisers"* were purchased for flights to New York, followed by the de Havilland Comet in 1952. Los Angeles was added to the extensive worldwide route network in March 1961, with *"over-the-pole flights"* from London Heathrow, using Boeing 707s. The airline received its first Boeing 747 aircraft for long-haul service in 1971, and a year later, was renamed British Airways. By 1980, British Airways was flying a daily, non-stop service between Los Angeles and London, using the Boeing 747s. Rolling out on Runway 25 Left after having landed is G-BDXD, a Boeing 747-236B.

December 1980

VARIG Brasil airline's predecessor, Redes Estaduais Aereas Ltda. (REAL) Brasil, was one of a handful of international carriers that started service into Los Angeles during the decade of the 1950s. During 1958, REAL Brasil acquired four Lockheed L-1049H Super Constellation aircraft to expand its international services. Los Angeles was added to the network in 1959, with a weekly, multi-stop, Rio de Janeiro-Brasilia-Manaus-Bogotá-Mexico City-Los Angeles flight. In May 1960, REAL added Tokyo, from Rio via Los Angeles, then through Honolulu and Wake Island. This seven stop service between Rio de Janerio and Tokyo was one of the longest in the world at that time and took a week for the round-trip journey. In 1961, VARIG took ownership of REAL and assumed its operations. With the purchase of new Douglas DC-10 aircraft in 1972, VARIG was able to serve Los Angeles with a one-stop service to Rio de Janeiro. Awaiting takeoff clearance on a bright winter morning is PP-VMW, a Douglas DC-10-30.

December 1980

Trans-Texas Airways became the airline of the Lone Star State in July 1947, when service was started between Houston and Dallas, using Douglas DC-3s. The small airline expanded past its Texan borders in 1955, with flights into Arkansas and Louisiana. In 1966, the airline placed its first jet powered aircraft in service, a Douglas DC-9, to provide *"Pamper Jet"* service on the more important routes. During 1968, the airline changed its name to Texas International, reflecting the introduction of a new route to Monterrey, Mexico and the growing status of the carrier. Two years later, in January 1970, the airline started daily service into Los Angeles from Albuquerque, New Mexico. The airline's *"Peanuts Fares"* made the flights popular and affordable amongst travelers until 1982, when a new holding company was formed known as Texas Air, which merged Texas International into Continental Airlines. Preparing to push-back from the gate at Terminal 6 for a mid-day flight is N8901E, a Douglas DC-9-14.

September 1980

The de Havilland DHC-6 Twin Otter was the workhorse of the Golden West fleet and was the aircraft that the airline developed operations with during its formation in May 1969. The Short-Takeoff-Or-Landing (STOL) airplane permitted the airline to serve smaller, regional Southern California airports, such as Fullerton, Riverside, Palmdale, and Inyokern. The aircraft was perfect for the short-haul, low-passenger flights and allowed the airline to serve markets that were uneconomical with its larger aircraft. The fleet of twelve Twin Otter airplanes were a common sight at Los Angeles, where Golden West flew to ten cities, many of these flights to the smaller desert communities where the DHC-6 was welcome. Although the larger Shorts 330 and DHC-7 replaced the Twin Otter on some services in the early 1980s, they continued to fly the *"thinner"* routes until the airlines demise in April 1983. Parked at the commuter ramp, once located on the west side of the airport, is N66180, a de Havilland DHC-6-200.

September 1980

When millionaire Howard Hughes and his Summa Corporation purchased AirWest in 1970, the new owner decided to rebrand the airline Hughes Airwest and introduced a vibrant yellow color scheme. The colorful new jets quickly became known as the *"Flying Bananas."* Over the next ten years, the airline established itself as a large, regional carrier, operating hundreds of daily flights to over forty-two cities; from Edmonton, Canada, in the north, south to Manzanillo, Mexico and east to Milwaukee. The airline's fleet of forty-five Douglas DC-9 aircraft flew the majority of services across the network with an additional six Boeing 727s covering the longer routes. By 1980, the airline was serving twelve cities from Los Angeles including Palm Springs, Tucson, and Spokane. Republic Airlines purchased Hughes Airwest for $38.5 million in October 1980, bringing an end to the legendary carrier. Seen only a month before its purchase and taxiing inbound towards its gate at Terminal 6 is N9331, a Douglas DC-9-31.

July 1980
As its name suggested, Aspen Airways was founded in 1953, in the mountain resort town of Aspen, Colorado, as a local air-taxi operator. Daily Denver-Aspen service was started in 1962, for which the new airline provided the only airline link between the City of Aspen and Denver, thus allowing travel time over the traditional highway route to be cut in half. The airline would remain an intra-Colorado carrier through the 1970s, until 1980, when authority was received to operate flights in California. The airline relocated some of its Convair 580s west and focused on daily flights to the California mountain resort of Lake Tahoe, from cities such as Los Angeles, Burbank, and San Francisco. Growth continued and in 1982, a non-stop Los Angeles-Aspen flight was added, which was quite popular during the winter ski season. Due to restructuring and after only three years of service, Aspen Airways terminated its California operations. Holding short of Runway 24 Left for a morning departure is N5809, a Convair 580.

April 1980
Aeromexico, the national flag carrier of Mexico, was founded in 1934, as Aeronaves de Mexico. In 1961, the airline assumed operation of smaller carriers including Guest Aerovias and LAMSA, then changed its name to Aeromexico in 1972, and introduced a new, vibrant color scheme. Aeronaves de Mexico was the original operator into Los Angeles, starting service in late 1962, with a flight to Guadalajara via Tijuana using a Douglas DC-6. As the jet-age dawned, Aeromexico became a loyal Douglas customer, ordering both the Douglas DC-8 for long-haul operations and the Douglas DC-9 for short and medium range services. With the introduction of jet aircraft, additional routes from Los Angeles to various Mexican resort destinations were started and by the early 1980s, the smaller DC-9 was providing flights to Guadalajara, Tijuana, and Monterrey, while the DC-8 was still flying the popular Los Angeles-Mexico City route. Starting its takeoff roll on Runway 24 Left is XA-SIB *"Jalisco,"* a Douglas DC-8-51.

April 1980
Swift Aire started operations in March 1969, from a Central California base of San Luis Obispo, flying daily flights to both Sacramento and San Francisco. Los Angeles was added a few months later, with non-stop flights to San Luis Obispo, using a Piper Navajo airplane. As demand for service increased, the airline added some unique aircraft to operate new routes, including the de Havilland Heron and the Aérospatiale Nord 262. Three Fokker F-27 *"Friendship"* aircraft were purchased in 1979, with the first plane being delivered in January 1980. The new 56-passenger turboprops were immediately put into the popular services from Los Angeles and within a few months, the airline added additional flights from LAX to Santa Maria, San Luis Obispo, Sacramento, and Bakersfield. Only a year later, in 1981, was Swift Aire was purchased and absorbed by the newly established commuter, Golden Gate Airlines. Holding short of Runway 24 Left on a pleasant spring morning is N421SA, a Fokker F-27-600.

March 1980

Cochise Airlines was one of the first carriers to receive official *"Commuter"* certification by the Civil Aeronautics Board (CAB), when it was established in 1971. Based in Tucson, Arizona, the small airline focused on under-served Arizona airports before starting service to the West Coast in early 1979. Five daily flights were added to Los Angeles along a multi-stop route connecting Phoenix, Arizona, via Yuma and El Centro-Imperial. During this time, Cochise found itself competing with similar commuter airline Sun Aire, which had started non-stop service from Los Angeles to both El Centro-Imperial and Yuma as well. Only a few years later would financial problems result in scheduled passenger services being cut, with the airline then only focusing on charter flights before finally ceasing all operations in June 1982. Parked at the original commuter ramp, located on the west side of the airport and awaiting taxi clearance for another eastbound flight is N24AZ, a Swearingen SA-226TC Metro II.

March 1981

Trans World Airlines (TWA) was one of the first air carriers to start service into Los Angeles when predecessor, Transcontinental & Western Air started a multi-stop, transcontinental, Los Angeles-New York service in 1930, using Ford Tri-Motor airplanes. By 1963, TWA was flying to twelve destinations from LAX including, New York, Boston, Philadelphia, Phoenix, and Paris, France. TWA used Los Angeles as a focal point in its growing network and the city became host to numerous inaugural flights of the airline's new Boeing 747 and Lockheed L-1011s. In the late 1970s, TWA purchased three 747SPs for anticipated service to the Middle East, however these routes were declined. The long-range Jumbos were used instead on both transcontinental and trans-Atlantic flights such as from Los Angeles to Boston, New York, and London, England, before being removed from service a few years later. Holding short of the Runway 24 Left for a morning departure to the Big Apple is N58201, a Boeing 747SP-31.

April 1981
Destined to become one of the world's largest express freight carriers, with the popular 1980s catch slogan, *"When it absolutely, positively has to be there overnight,"* Federal Express started with humble beginnings in 1973, from a base in Memphis, Tennessee. Early operations used a fleet of Dassault Falcon jets for charter freight and airmail services. In 1978, deregulation of the air cargo industry took place, which allowed Federal Express to greatly expand and add the Boeing 727 for its small and medium package loads and the Douglas DC-10 for its larger volume flights. By 1981, the airline had grown into the largest overnight package company in the world and was serving one hundred cities in the United States and two in Canada. Due to the large market and package quantity, Los Angeles was one of the first airports to be served with the airlines trademark purple and crimson painted DC-10s. Parked at the south cargo ramp and awaiting a flight later that evening is N68055, a Douglas DC-10-10F.

May 1981

The national flag carrier of Finland, Finnair, is one of the oldest continuously operated airlines in the world, having been established in 1923. Early flights of the Nordic carrier connected the capital of Finland, Helsinki, with neighboring Stockholm, Sweden and Tallinn, Estonia. After World War II, Finnair purchased a Douglas DC-3, and resumed flights, adding more cities in northern Europe. Finnair was a loyal Douglas customer and orders for two intercontinental range DC-8 aircraft allowed the airline to expand across the Atlantic and start flights into New York in 1969. Finnair continued a trend of steady growth and eventually purchased two Douglas DC-10 airplanes for long-range services on trans-Atlantic flights. In May 1981, Finnair finally extending its reach to the Pacific Coast and started twice-weekly flights between Helsinki and Los Angeles via Seattle, using the Douglas DC-10. Seen being prepared to be pulled into the gate at Terminal 7 is OH-LHA *"Iso Antti,"* a Douglas DC-10-30.

June 1981

Golden Gate Airlines was another new commuter airline that was formed on January 16, 1980, as the result of the merger of three smaller carriers; Air Pacific and Swift Aire both from California and Gem State Airlines of Idaho. The new airline operated a variety of equipment due to the merger, including the Convair 580, de Havilland DHC-7 *"Dash 7"* and Swearingen Metroliner. Los Angeles was one of the first cities to be served by the new carrier with non-stop flights to both Modesto and Monterey. The airline quickly grew into a respected regional carrier, serving twenty cities in six states, with over 1,300 flights a week. New flights were started in early 1981, which connected Los Angeles to the California Central Valley cities of Fresno, Bakersfield, and Stockton. Due to the rapid growth, the airline eventually suffered mounting financial difficulties and filed for bankruptcy in August 1981, only a year-and-a-half after inaugurating service. Parked at Terminal 7 is N701GG, a de Havilland DHC-7-102.

August 1981

Delta Airlines started from modest beginnings in 1924, as a crop dusting service based in Macon, Georgia. Passenger services started in 1929, between Jackson, Mississippi and Dallas, Texas using a Travel Air S-6000-B aircraft. Delta Airlines remained focused on the southeastern region of the United States, but had ambitions to fly routes farther west. During the 1950s, Delta established service to Los Angeles, but only through interline-route agreements with other airlines. Finally, in June 1961, Delta started its own service to Los Angeles with non-stop flights to Atlanta, Dallas, and New Orleans using the Douglas DC-8. Delta became one of the few airlines that ordered the Lockheed L-1011 *"Tristar"* airplane, with the first of twenty-four being delivered in 1973. The new-wide body aircraft were soon placed on Delta's popular routes from LAX to Atlanta, Dallas, New Orleans, and San Francisco. At the hold-short point, for Runway 24 Left on an overcast summer morning is N1732D, a Lockheed L-1011-1.

October 1981

American Airlines was one of the first airlines to place an order for the new Boeing 747 aircraft in the late 1960s, planning to use the *"Jumbo Jet"* on both heavy domestic and long trans-Pacific services. Dubbed the *"AstroLiner,"* American's first Boeing 747-100 was put into service between Los Angeles and New York on March 2, 1970. American soon realized that the plane's 361-seats were hard to keep filled and replaced fifty of the seats in the coach cabin with a lounge complete with an electric piano. Even while flying their new *"LuxuryLiners"* between heavily travelled domestic routes, American found the only profitable route for the 747 was between Los Angeles and New York City. American Airlines soon withdrew the planes from service, converted them to pure freighters and by 1984, all of American's fourteen Boeing 747s had been removed from passenger service. Moving east along Taxiway Uniform toward Runway 24 Left for a morning departure to New York City is N9664, a Boeing 747-123.

November 1981
Braniff International Airways was established in 1928, to provide passenger service between Tulsa and Oklahoma City with a Stinson airplane. In 1946, Braniff was awarded routes to South America, followed by the purchase of Panagra Airlines in 1967, further solidifying Braniff's South American presence. Braniff assumed the flights from Los Angeles to Bogotá, Columbia and Lima, Peru, started by Panagra in 1966. After deregulation in 1978, the airline expanded both internationally and domestically, becoming a trendy and well-known carrier. In the early 1980s, Los Angeles continued to be connected to the South American cities of Lima, Peru, Bogotá, Colombia, and Santiago, Chile, with the DC-8, while the Boeing 727 flew to San Francisco and Dallas. Due to pending debt and continuing losses, Braniff went bankrupt in May 1982, suspending operations of one of the largest airlines in the U.S. Holding short of Runway 24 Left is N434BN, a Boeing 727-227, in the legendary *"Flying Colors"* scheme.

November 1981
Based at Los Angeles, Western Airlines, one of the largest carriers at the airport, started operations on July 13, 1925, as Western Air Express, flying a mail contract between Los Angeles and Salt Lake City. Passenger operations commenced a year later, on the same route, with a Fokker F-10 Tri-Motor airplane. The airline remained relatively small until 1941, when new routes were added, Douglas DC-3s were purchased, and its name changed to Western Airlines. The Boeing 737-200 was added to the fleet in 1968, and allowed for pure *"jet"* service to be provided to smaller cities in the network such as, Boise, Idaho, Casper, Wyoming, and Helena, Montana. The series-200 was used extensively in the Los Angeles market to serve a variety of routes, including flights to competitive markets such as San Francisco and Phoenix, as well as regional services to cities such as, Albuquerque and Fresno. At the hold-short point for Runway 24 Left and wearing the famous *"swizzle-stick"* livery is N4520W, a Boeing 737-247.

August 1982
Transamerica was started as Los Angeles Airways in 1948, flying a single Douglas DC-3 for contract cargo and freight service. In 1960, the airline became Trans International and expanded its business to include passenger, military, and government charters. During 1976, the airline acquired the large charter carrier, Saturn Airways, and became the world's largest charter airline. The airline changed its name again, to reflect its parent company, Transamerica Corporation, and in May 1979, the carrier received authority for scheduled passenger operations between New York City and Europe. Scheduled services to Los Angeles started in 1981, with flights to Shannon, Ireland, and both Dallas and Honolulu using Douglas DC-8s and Boeing 747s. Transamerica was a familiar sight at Los Angeles for both scheduled and chartered flights until increased costs and labor issues forced the airline to suspend operations in September 1986. Being towed to the airport west pads for holding is N4865T, a Douglas DC-8-73CF.

October 1982

Capitol Airlines was formed in 1946, to provide military contract work and passenger charter operations, initially utilizing Douglas DC-3 aircraft. The airline grew to become one of the largest charter operators in the U.S. and focused a majority of its efforts on tour group packages to points in Europe from the United States. In 1978, the airline was granted authority to provide scheduled flights and one of the first routes started was the popular Los Angeles to New York service using Douglas DC-8s. Three *"Wide-Body"* Douglas DC-10s were then leased to provide the famous *"$ky $aver"* service, which guaranteed low fares between Los Angeles, New York, and Chicago. Scheduled flights also connected other U.S. cities with points in Europe and the Caribbean. The airline, which had been operating at a loss continually since 1975, went through some business changes before filing for bankruptcy in November 1984. Preparing to take Runway 24 Left for a morning departure is N917CL, a Douglas DC-10-10.

November 1982

Republic Airlines was formed on July 1, 1979, with the merger of two regional carriers; Southern Airways and North Central Airlines. The combined operation of the new airline had all of its routes focused on the region east of the Rocky Mountains, however, Republic sought expansion westward. The answer came in the purchase of Hughes Airwest on October 1, 1980. With the acquisition of Hughes Airwest, Republic Airlines truly became a national carrier and grew to serve over 150 destinations across the United States, Mexico, Canada, and the Cayman Islands. The Douglas DC-9 was the foundation of the fleet with the airline operating over 130 of the planes making it the largest operator of the type worldwide. Los Angeles benefited from the Republic Airlines growth as the airline continued flying most of the original Hughes Airwest routes and added new cities to the east. Holding short of Runway 24 Left and proudly displaying the famed *"Herman"* logo is N9348, a Douglas DC-9-15.

December 1982

Another result of the Airline Deregulation Act of 1978, was Muse Air, whose name reflects its founder Lamar Muse, once president and CEO of Southwest Airlines. Muse Air provided one-class service with all leather seating and a no-smoking policy, using two newly delivered, McDonnell Douglas MD-80 airplanes. Flights started in July 1981, from its base at Houston Hobby to Dallas Love Field, both in Texas. With sights to the west, Los Angeles was added in October 1982, with non-stop service to Houston. Further expansion continued with Austin, San Antonio, Las Vegas, and San Diego being flown from Los Angeles with both Douglas DC-9s and *"Super 80s."* Even with controlled expansion, the airline was losing money and looking for a potential buyer. Ironically, Muse Air was purchased by Southwest Airlines, which changed the airline's name to Transtar Airlines in early 1986. Preparing to depart Runway 25 Left for an evening flight to Houston is N930MC, a McDonnell Douglas DC-9-82 (MD-82).

February 1983
Northwest Airlines started modestly in 1926, flying a government mail contract between Minneapolis and Chicago. By 1935, the airline had expanded west to Seattle and connected numerous cities along the northwestern half of the United States. Military contract flights across the Pacific spurred the airline's commercial passenger service to the Far East and by 1969, Northwest had such a large presence in Japan and Korea that *"Orient"* was added to its title. The airline's first Boeing 747 was delivered in 1970, and was a welcome addition to the growing trans-Pacific network. Los Angeles was added to the airline's route map in October 1969, with flights to Minneapolis and a few months later, Tokyo service was started via Honolulu using the new 747 *"Jumbo Jet."* By 1983, the airline was flying daily Tokyo flights from Los Angeles with its 747s, as well as, non-stop flights to Seattle, San Diego, Honolulu, and Minneapolis. Taxiing inbound toward the terminal after a morning arrival is N611US, a Boeing 747-251B.

February 1983

Based in Chico, California, Pacific Express Airlines was started in April 1981, to provide low-cost jet service to points in California, Oregon, and Idaho. Unique amongst start-up carriers during the time, the airline chose to utilize the British made short-range airliner, the British Aerospace BAC-1-11. Early service connected the various San Francisco Bay area airports with the desert resort city of Palm Springs, followed by service to Los Angeles in April 1982. The airline rapidly expanded, eventually serving eight cities from Los Angeles including Palm Springs, Las Vegas, Fresno, and Modesto. The airline, keeping with its British loyalty, ordered fourteen of the new British Aerospace BAe 146 airplanes, and proposed adding eleven new cities across the West. Due to deepening financial issues, the airline could not secure additional funding and halted operations in May 1984. Taxiing eastbound along Taxiway Uniform toward its gate at Terminal 2 after having landed is N106EX, a British Aerospace BAC 1-11-201AC.

June 1983
One of the more popular airline destinations from Los Angeles during the 1980s, was to Honolulu, Hawaii. Although this route was traditionally flown by major carriers such as Western Airline's *"Islander"* and United Airline's *"Royal Hawaiian"* flights, deregulation brought new airlines to the market. The Hawaii Express was formed in August 1982, to provide affordable flights in the Honolulu market and started Los Angeles-Honolulu service using a leased Boeing 747 airplane. In May 1983, the airline leased two Douglas DC-10s to replace the sole 747 and planned to expand services to San Francisco. Even though the airline was providing deeply discounted fares, the competing carriers easily matched the prices and within months, drove The Hawaii Express into bankruptcy. In December 1983, the airline ceased operations and the colorful, pineapple clad aircraft were returned to the lessors. Making its way along Taxiway Uniform toward Terminal 3 after having landed is N904WA, a Douglas DC-10-10.

July 1983

What started as a flight school and air taxi operator based at Santa Monica airport just north of Los Angeles in 1978, evolved to become scheduled commuter Wings West Airlines. Services commenced a year later, in November 1979, using Cessna 402 aircraft. With the addition of Metro turboprop equipment in 1983, the airline expanded its route structure and moved its base of operations to San Luis Obispo in central California. Assuming many of the Essential Air Service routes given up through deregulation, Wings West grew to become one of the largest commuter airlines in California, flying to fourteen cities within the state. Los Angeles alone, was served with over fifty daily flights, to eight cities, including Visalia, Santa Maria, Oxnard, Modesto, and Merced. During June 1986, Wings West became an American Eagle affiliate and was then eventually purchased by American Airlines in 1987. Approaching Runway 25 Right for an evening departure is N31107, a Fairchild Swearingen SA-227AC Metro III.

August 1983

Korean Airlines was established in 1962, to replace the former government owned airline; Korean National Airlines. Early routes connected Seoul to neighboring countries such as Japan and Vietnam. Seeking trans-Pacific service, the airline ordered two, new Boeing 747 airplanes, the first being delivered in May 1973. The new plane was put into service flying a Los Angeles-Seoul route via Honolulu and Tokyo. Pleased with the performance of the 747, the airline placed an order for the new Special Performance version of the legendary aircraft in 1979. When delivered to the airline in 1981, the Boeing 747SP was initially used on the 6,900-mile, non-stop, New York-Seoul route, thereby eliminating the Anchorage technical stop. The Boeing 747SP was then placed on non-stop service between Los Angeles and Seoul in late 1981, supplementing the existing multi-stop, trans-Pacific route. Having just landed and enroute to the international arrivals concourse at Terminal 2 is HL7457, a Boeing 747SP-B5.

August 1983

Singapore Airlines was the government owned airline of Singapore and was formed with the break-up of Malaysia Singapore Airlines (MSA) in October 1972. Some of the original MSA routes and operation of aircraft continued, yet the new Singapore Airlines ordered new airplanes and opened up new domestic and international routes. The airline received its first Boeing 747 in the summer of 1973, and the new *"Jumbo"* was used to add distance and capacity on routes to Europe and the Far East. In 1977, the airline started trans-Pacific services by adding Honolulu, San Francisco, and Los Angeles to its international network. Flights from Los Angeles to Singapore were routed via Honolulu then Taipei or Tokyo. In 1983, when the airline took delivery of its first, 416-passenger, Boeing 747-300 *"Big Top,"* it was quickly placed on the popular, long-haul, international services to the U.S. West Coast. Taxiing inbound toward international arrivals at Terminal 2 after a long trans-Pacific flight is 9V-SKA, a Boeing 747-312.

September 1983
Los Angeles was one of the first cities America West Airlines added to its route structure when operations commenced on August 1, 1983. The new airline's philosophy was to provide high-frequency, low-cost service from a centralized Phoenix, Arizona hub. The airline quickly grew and within two years was serving twenty-three cities within the Midwest and West Coast regions of the United States, as well as Edmonton, Canada. The Boeing 737-200 provided the foundation of the airline's fleet and it was a natural decision when an initial order was placed for two of the new, fuel-effecient, Boeing 737-300 aircraft. During the 1980s, America West only served Los Angeles from Phoenix and Las Vegas, not wanting to face stiff competition in other established markets. The airline was able to prosper through the difficult decade of the 1980s as a well known and respected carrier. Having just been pushed back from the gate at Terminal 4 and awaiting taxi clearance is N128AW, a Boeing 737-275.

February 1984
After having flown for almost ten years in its small desert market, Sun Aire finally gained approval to start service into Los Angeles in 1977, with flights to Palm Springs. Using Swearingen Metroliners, in direct competition with major carriers, American Airlines and Hughes Airwest's jet flights, the little commuter was able to survive the *"Big Guys."* Sun Aire continued to add flights from Los Angeles, starting service to El Centro-Imperial later that year. By the early 1980s, Sun Aire established itself as a reliable commuter carrier and soon formed a hub operation out of the growing Los Angeles market. By 1984, the airline had over seventy daily flights from LAX and served eleven cities, including Santa Barbara, Palm Springs, El Centro, and Yuma. The airline continued to be a major commuter carrier from Los Angeles serving as the *"Desert Connection,"* until its purchase by SkyWest Airlines in September 1985. Parked at the Terminal 4 commuter ramp is N1010Z, a Swearingen SA-226TC Metro II.

February 1984

Trans Canada Airlines (TCA) was formed by the Canadian government in 1937, with a small, domestic route structure and an international flight between Vancouver and Seattle. In 1965, TCA became Air Canada and in 1967, Los Angeles was added to the airlines growing international network, utilizing the Douglas DC-8 on non-stop flights to Toronto. The Douglas DC-8 had replaced the piston engine aircraft and increased speed and comfort on both trans-Atlantic and domestic routes. Air Canada became the first, non-U.S. airline, to put the Lockheed L-1011 in service in 1973, mainly on dense domestic flights, and North American and trans-Atlantic routings. In 1975, the L-1011 was supplementing the Boeing 747 and 727 on the airline's popular, Los Angeles-Toronto *"Maple Leaf"* service. By 1984, Air Canada had daily, non-stop flights between Los Angeles and Toronto, Calgary, and Montréal, Canada. Rotating for takeoff on Runway 24 Left enroute to Toronto is C-FTND, a Lockheed L-1011-1 Tristar.

April 1984
One of the first attempts to cater to the growing trend of business class customers was Air 1, which was established in 1981. The new airline focused on providing business class service at coach prices, from its base in St. Louis, to various points in the United States. The airline leased four Boeing 727s and had each aircraft fitted with a first class layout having a capacity of only sixty-eight passengers. In-flight services included complimentary wines, telephones, and multi-course meals. Scheduled flights finally started on April 1, 1983, from St. Louis to Dallas, Kansas City, Newark, and Washington Dulles. Although the new airline struggled to fill its seats, new services were started to Los Angeles from St. Louis in April 1984, hoping to attract business travelers in that popular market. With continuing losses, the airline was eventually forced to declare bankruptcy and suspended operations in October 1984. On short final and *"over-the-numbers"* for landing on Runway 25 Left is N4612, a Boeing 727-35.

June 1984
With the passing of the Airline Deregulation Act in 1978, many new airlines were formed, including numerous commuters hoping to fill the void of serving the smaller cities and communities that the larger airlines had abandoned. California was no exception and over twenty new airlines were started in the state alone during the early 1980s, many assuming the original Essential Air Service routes flown prior to deregulation. One of the more colorful, yet short-lived commuter airlines was Connect Air, which was established in April 1984. The new airline provided scheduled services from a base in Santa Barbara to both Los Angeles and San Jose, California, and Las Vegas, Nevada. Connect Air leased two Fairchild F-27 turboprops with a capacity of forty-four passengers for its flights. Unfortunately, competition and lack of solid finances resulted in the airline suspending operations only a few months later in August 1984. Parked at Terminal 3 in its vibrant color scheme is N1823L, a Fairchild F-27A.

June 1984

Based at London Gatwick Airport and formed by the merger of British United Airways (BUA) and Caledonian Airways in 1970, the new airline, British Caledonian Airlines or BCAL, would become the second major British airline to provide flights on worldwide routes. The previous airline, BUA, had extensive routes in Europe, Africa, and South America, while Caledonian focused on holiday charter flights. The new BCAL sought flights to the West Coast of the U.S. and started service to Los Angeles in April 1973, using Boeing 707s. Due to economic issues, this route was dropped only a year later in 1974. Service to Los Angeles from London Gatwick didn't resume again until May 1982, when BCAL assumed operation of the ex-Laker Airways route. Depending on passenger loads, both Boeing 747 and Douglas DC-10 aircraft were used on the non-stop services. Taxiing toward Runway 25 Right for an evening departure is G-BHDJ, named *"James S. McDonnell,"* a fitting tribute to this McDonnell Douglas DC-10-30.

June 1984

Imperial Airlines was a small, local airline started in 1964, as Visco Flying Service, to provide flights between San Diego and the desert community of El Centro using Beech 18 aircraft. In 1979, the airline changed ownership, moved its base of operations to Carlsbad (just north of San Diego) and became known as Imperial Commuter Airlines. During 1980, with the introduction of the Embraer EMB-110 Bandeirante *"Jet-Prop,"* the airline added Los Angeles to its route network with flights to Carlsbad, Fullerton, and Riverside. Imperial Airlines quickly grew and eventually made Los Angeles its hub of operations and by 1984, the airline was serving eight destinations from LAX including Orange County, Bakersfield, Carlsbad, and Ontario. With the purchase of three Shorts 360 turboprop aircraft, Imperial was able to promote its popular *"Freeway Flyer"* service between Los Angeles and San Diego until 1986, when the airline was forced into bankruptcy. Taxiing outbound for takeoff is N601A, a Shorts SD-360-100.

June 1984

The major airline of the Middle Eastern country of Jordan, Alia Royal Jordanian, was established in December of 1963, when King Hussein authorized the formation of the airline to succeed the existing Jordan Airways. The new airline acquired Douglas DC-7 and Caravelle aircraft to fly scheduled services from Amman to neighboring countries, including Egypt and Israel. The government took ownership of the airline in 1968, and subsequently purchased Boeing 707 and 720 equipment in 1971. Two Boeing 747 airplanes were delivered in 1977, for services across the North Atlantic to New York City. By 1981, additional cities in the United States were added to the route network, including both Chicago and Houston. New services to Los Angeles were inaugurated in March 1984, with flights to Amman via Chicago then Amsterdam using either Lockheed L-1011 and Boeing 747 aircraft. Awaiting push back from the newly built International Terminal is JY-AFB *"Princess Haya,"* a Boeing 747-2D3B Combi.

July 1984
The national airline of New Zealand was originally formed in 1940, as Tasman Empire Airways Ltd., flying between Auckland and Sydney, with Short S.30 flying boats. As the local airline extended its wings over routes in the Southern Pacific, its name was changed to Air New Zealand and its assets were purchased by the government in 1961. During this time, the airline was operating Douglas DC-4 and Lockheed Electra equipment on its routes to Australia and various Southern Pacific islands. In July 1965, Air New Zealand placed its first jet airliner, a Douglas DC-8-52, into service and four months later trans-Pacific service commenced to Los Angeles. In 1973, Douglas DC-10s were placed on the route and in 1981, the airline's first Boeing 747 was put into service, connecting Los Angeles to both London and Auckland via Honolulu or Papeete. Lining up on Runway 25 Right for an early evening flight across the Pacific and displaying the tribal Maori *"Kora"* symbol is ZK-NZZ *"Tokomaru,"* a Boeing 747-219B.

July 1984
Serving the Pacific island state of Hawaii, Hawaiian Airlines was started as Inter-Island Airways in 1929, using Sikorsky S-38 amphibian boats on various *"island-hopping"* flights. In 1941, after purchasing a Douglas DC-3 for passenger service, the small carrier changed its name to Hawaiian Airlines. Douglas DC-9 airplanes brought *"jet"* service to the islands in 1966, and provided quicker, more reliable schedules. The airline remained intra-island, mainly due to its remote Pacific location, until December 1983, when the airline leased three, Douglas DC-8s for worldwide charter service. Most of its charter work focused on tour group flights from cities along the U.S. West Coast to Honolulu. Scheduled services to the U.S. Mainland finally commenced in June 1985, with Los Angeles-Honolulu flights, followed a few months later by expansion to San Francisco and Seattle. Having just taken the active Runway 25 Right for an evening charter flight back to the island paradise is N802BN, a Douglas DC-8-62H.

September 1984

PEOPLExpress was considered an early success of deregulation when the low-fare airline started flights in April 1981. Based at Newark Airport, PEOPLExpress, using the Boeing 737, connected the population of the New York area with points along the Eastern Seaboard and Florida. The airline quickly expanded to cities in the Midwest and Texas, then started trans-Atlantic service to London. In early 1984, transcontinental flights commenced connecting Newark to Los Angeles, using the high-capacity Boeing 747. Los Angeles was served with three daily flights, and with fares as low as $129, one-way, kept the competition tense in the infamous Los Angeles-New York market. After some troubling finances in the mid-1980s, the airline acquired Frontier Airlines in 1985. The operation of both carriers, losing money together, finally forced the airline to file bankruptcy and be taken over by Texas Air in February 1987. Preparing to take Runway 24 Left for a mid-day departure to Newark is N604PE, a Boeing 747-243B.

September 1984

The national airline of Italy, Aerolinee Italiane Internazionali, was established in 1946, by the Italian government and British European Airways. In 1957, following a merger with competing Italian carrier Linee Aeree Italiane, the new airline became the country's flag carrier, known as Alitalia. The airline's presence soon spread throughout Europe, followed by intercontinental routes to Africa, the Middle East, and Far East. Service across the North Atlantic to North America started in 1960, with Douglas DC-8 flights to New York. Additional cities including Chicago, Toronto, and Boston were added in the early 1970s using newly delivered Boeing 747 and Douglas DC-10 long-range aircraft. Alitalia added Los Angeles to its international network in March 1984, when *"Jumbo Jet"* services were extended on the Rome-Milan-Chicago route. Parked at the new International Terminal in the familiar national colors is I-DEMS *"Monte Argentario,"* a Boeing 747-243B, delivered to the airline just seven months earlier.

September 1984
In 1946, three Scandinavian countries, Denmark, Norway, and Sweden merged their national airlines together forming Scandinavian Airlines System (SAS) to better manage and promote passenger air service. In 1954, SAS was the first airline to establish an *"over-the-pole"* route, when service was started from Copenhagen to Los Angeles, via Søndre Strømfjord, Greenland, and Winnipeg, Canada, using a Douglas DC-7C aircraft. The piston powered airplanes were eventually replaced with the Douglas DC-8 in the early 1960s. In 1971, SAS placed the Boeing 747 into service on longer range routes to North America and Asia, allowing an increase in distance and passengers/cargo carried. With the addition of the 747 and McDonnell Douglas DC-10, SAS was able to start non-stop services from Copenhagen to Los Angeles, using much of the same pioneering polar route it had established years earlier. Rolling out on Runway 24 Left after landing is LN-AEO *"Ivar Viking,"* a Boeing 747-283B.

November 1984

After the bankruptcy and eventual shut down of Braniff International Airways in 1982, the Hyatt Corporation sought to resurrect the legacy carrier under a new operating philosophy. The *"new"* Braniff would be based at Dallas-Ft. Worth, Texas, and initially fly to eighteen cities across the United States using a fleet of thirty, leased Boeing 727 airplanes. Service started in March 1984, from Dallas, with Los Angeles being one of the inaugural cities. Within a few years, a secondary hub was established in Kansas City and daily flights were started to Los Angeles and five additional cities. Braniff became a popular choice for passengers from Los Angeles due to low fares and reputable service through the late 1980s. The airline was a familiar sight at LAX, until September 1989, when due to poor business decisions and operating economics, Braniff filed for bankruptcy and suspended operations a month later. Holding in position and awaiting takeoff clearance on Runway 25 Left is N469BN, a Boeing 727-227.

December 1984

After a bitter battle to determine whether Airbus or Boeing would supply the aircraft required for the airline's medium range requirements, Trans World Airlines (TWA) decided to order ten Boeing 767 airplanes in December 1979. The airline's first 767 was delivered on November 11, 1982, and service was inaugurated a few weeks later on a Los Angeles-Washington Dulles route. After only a few months of service, TWA was quick to realize the aircraft's fuel efficiency and cost savings on transcontinental flights and soon replaced the traditional Boeing 747 service with the new *"Twin-Jet"* on both the popular Los Angeles-New York and Los Angeles-St. Louis routes. TWA would eventually acquire twenty-two 767 airplanes, including the stretch, series-300 and became the first U.S. airline to start trans-Atlantic, twin-engine operations to Europe in February 1985. Lining up on Runway 24 Left for an early evening departure is N602TW, a Boeing 767-231(ER), and the second example to be delivered to the airline.

December 1984
The national airline for the South American country of Argentina was established in May 1949, with the merger of four regional airlines. Services to North America were started in 1950, using the Douglas DC-6 on flights to New York City. The airline was an early operator of the luxurious de Havilland Comet and used the aircraft to start jet flights to Europe and New York City in 1959. The airline placed the Boeing 707 into service in 1966, eventually replacing the Comets and providing the airline with a solid aircraft for further expansion. Flights to Los Angeles was started in June 1969, using the Boeing 707 on a multi-stop, Buenos Aires-Lima-Bogotá-Mexico City-Los Angeles routing. As the airline continued to grow, it placed an order for three, Boeing 747 airplanes in 1978, to be used on the higher capacity, long-range routes to both Europe and North America, including the popular services to LAX. Seen *"over-the-numbers"* of Runway 25 Left during an early morning arrival is LV-OOZ, a Boeing 747-287B.

January 1985

Regent Air was the first passenger carrier to start the *"luxury"* first class airline service popular throughout the mid-to-late 1980s. Founded in Los Angeles as First Air, a name change a few years later to the more elegant Regent Air truly described the airline's two Boeing 727 airplanes. The aircraft were specially modified for a thirty-five passenger layout, with open leather seating and richly appointed interiors and fixtures. Service started in October 1984, with a daily, non-stop, Los Angeles-Newark flight. At a time when most other airlines were cutting transcontinental fares, Regent Air charged $1,620 (1985 dollars) for a one-way ticket. Although steep, that price included limousine transportation, gourmet in-flight meals, and an on-board secretary and beautician. Within a year however, the airline suffered huge financial losses and suspended operations in March 1986. Heading to Runway 25 Left, along Taxiway Foxtrot, in its *"classy"* gold and royal blue color scheme is N502RA, a Boeing 727-191.

February 1985

Frontier Airlines was created by the merger of three local airlines on June 1, 1950. The new airline initially focused its flights from Denver to the Rocky Mountain region and the southwest United States. In 1967, Frontier acquired Central Airlines of Texas, which allowed the airline to expand its route structure. As turboprop equipment was replaced by new *"Fan-Jet"* Boeing 727s in the late 1960s, Frontier extended its wings across the country. Service was launched to the U.S. West Coast when Los Angeles was added to the schedule in December 1980, with flights to both Denver and Salt Lake City. Flying the reliable, yet smaller Boeing 737, Frontier was faced with serious competition from traditional market carriers, United and Continental, flying their wide-body aircraft. Even after its purchase by PEOPLExpress in 1985, Frontier remained popular due to low fares and frequent flights, before eventually filing for bankruptcy in 1986. In position for takeoff on Runway 25 Left is N7399F, a Boeing 737-291.

February 1985
What started out as humble beginnings in 1967, as Air Southwest finally *"took-off"* four years later as Southwest Airlines in 1971, flying between Dallas Love Field, Houston, and San Antonio, Texas. In 1982, Southwest was granted authority to serve the U.S. West Coast from Texas, and one of the first cities to be added was Los Angeles, with flights to both San Antonio and Houston. Although ready to start service immediately, the airline was faced with a shortage of aircraft for the longer, higher capacity routes West. To remedy the situation, Southwest leased a total of six Boeing 727s from PEOPLExpress, with the aircraft being used on flights from points in Texas to Los Angeles, San Francisco, Phoenix, and San Diego. In 1984, the airline expanded at Los Angeles, adding new service to both El Paso and Phoenix, using the Boeing 737. By mid-1985, the 727s were returned with the arrival of the newer, fuel-efficient, longer range Boeing 737-300s. Holding short of Runway 24 Left is N564PE, a Boeing 727-227.

February 1985

Flying Tigers was historically one of the best known air freight companies and could trace its roots back to World War II, when an all-freight carrier was established in 1945, by ex-military pilots flying war surplus aircraft. Scheduled cargo service was started in the United States in 1949, from a base at Los Angeles, with flights to both San Francisco and Boston, using Douglas DC-4s. The airline continued to grow, acquiring more aircraft, additional routes, and cargo contracts. In 1965, Flying Tigers received its first *"jet"* airplane, a Boeing 707-349C, which increased range and speed of the larger cargo flights. During 1974, the airline became the first to operate a converted Boeing 747 *"Freighter"* on its popular cargo routes. In 1980, Flying Tigers purchased Seaboard World Airlines to become the world's largest freight carrier. Numerous daily flights to various points in the United States, Asia, and Europe were flown from its home base of LAX. In position for takeoff is N818FT, a Boeing 747-121, originally with Pan Am.

March 1985
When launched in 1964, Boeing's *"Baby"* 737 was never envisioned to become the world's best selling airliner. Designed for short-haul operations and to supplement the manufacturer's Boeing 727 and 707 product lines, German airline Lufthansa took delivery of the first series -100 in December 1967. United Airlines became the launch customer for the series-200, with improved gross weight and fuel capacity, ordering forty of the type, with their first aircraft being delivered in April 1968. The new aircraft were placed into service on short range routes throughout the United States, including flights within California from Los Angeles. Throughout the 1980s, United utilized the Boeing 737-200 from LAX to numerous regional destinations including San Francisco, Monterey, and Santa Barbara, California as well as Reno, Nevada. United Airlines would eventually operate over one-hundred of the successful 737s. Holding short of Runway 24 Left for a morning departure is N9040U, a Boeing 737-222.

March 1985
The national airline of Israel, El Al, was formed by the government in November 1948, with flights starting a year later in July 1949. The first flights covered a Tel Aviv-Rome-Paris route, using Douglas DC-4 aircraft. During 1961, the airline started trans-Atlantic service to New York, with Boeing 707 aircraft. El Al continued to grow and expand routes throughout Europe and North America during the late 1970s and early 1980s. In July 1983, El Al took delivery of a new Boeing 767 airplane, one of six ordered by the airline, to be used on longer, medium density services. The airline made history on March 27, 1984, when its Boeing 767 made a non-stop flight from Tel Aviv to Montréal, Canada, thus establishing the world's first passenger ETOPS (Extended Twin Overwater Passenger Service) route. Los Angeles was added to the network in the spring of 1984, as an extension of its Tel Aviv-Amsterdam-Chicago service. Seen *"over-the-numbers"* for landing on Runway 25 Left is 4X-EAD, a Boeing 767-258ER.

April 1985
During 1960, Trans Canadian Couriers was formed to provide small package and courier service to a limited area in both Ontario and Quebec, Canada. In 1967, Purolator, an American company well known for its automotive oil filters, purchased the company and continued to use the same name until 1973, when the name was changed to Purolator Courier. The courier company focused its efforts on small packages that could be delivered next day, using both ground vehicles and leased space on air carriers to provide this service. After the deregulation of the air cargo industry in 1978, Purolator took advantage and started its own "*airline*" in 1980, using both turboprop and jet aircraft leased from other companies. By 1984, the airline was using both Douglas DC-9 and Boeing 727 aircraft in full company colors, to fly thousands of packages overnight from major cities, including Los Angeles, to its hub at Indianapolis, Indiana. Parked at the south cargo ramp during a layover is N526PC, a Boeing 727-77C.

July 1985

During the early 1980s, Northwest Orient Airlines initiated a significant domestic route expansion program and sought a new narrow-body aircraft that would increase passenger loads and allow transcontinental routings. The airline placed a significant order for twenty of the new Boeing 757 airplanes in November 1983, as part of its fleet-wide enhancement strategy. The first, 184-passenger, Boeing 757 was delivered to the airline in February 1985, and was immediately placed on main-line routes from both Minneapolis-St. Paul and Detroit. Los Angeles was one of the first airports to host the new Boeing, with non-stop services to Detroit, followed by flights to Minneapolis. Northwest was so pleased with the performance and operating economics of the 757, that an additional ten aircraft were ordered to eventually replace the aging Boeing 727 fleet. Parked at Terminal 2 during a balmy summer evening turnaround is N501US *"City of St. Paul,"* a Boeing 757-251, and the first example delivered to the airline.

August 1985

The national airline of Spain, Líneas Aéreas de España SA, was formed in July 1940, to serve domestic routes within Spain, using Douglas DC-3 equipment. Within the next few years, international routes were started connecting Spain's capital of Madrid with Europe and South America. Service to the United States commenced in 1954, with flights to New York City using a Lockheed Super Constellation. Modern, long-range aircraft including the Boeing 747 and the Douglas DC-10, were delivered in the early 1970s, and allowed Iberia to expand its route network globally. During 1985, Iberia started seasonal summer service into Los Angeles with non-stop flights to Madrid, using the Boeing 747. Pleased with passenger loads, Iberia started year-round service to LAX in April 1987, continuing until code share agreements resulted in the airline discontinuing service to the airport in the 1990s. Approaching Runway 25 Right for departure on a sunny summer day is EC-DNP *"Juan Ramon Jimenez,"* a Boeing 747-256B.

August 1985

In 1942, the Canadian Pacific Railway Company merged ten local *"bush"* airlines to form Canadian Pacific Airlines, based in Vancouver, Canada. The new airline pioneered trans-Pacific routes for which the state-owned airline, Trans Canada Airlines (later Air Canada), did not deem profitable or viable. Flights to Sydney, Australia from Vancouver commenced in 1949, on a multi-stop route across the Pacific, using a Canadair CL-4 North Star airplane. Canadian Pacific continued to expand globally to Europe, South America, and the Orient, and in 1968, changed its operating name to CP Air. Los Angeles was added to the route network in April 1975, and a mix of Boeing 727 and 737 equipment was used on the daily, non-stop flights to Vancouver. CP Air was a regular visitor into Los Angeles until 1987, when a merger with Pacific Western Airlines resulted in the newly branded Canadian Airlines. On short final for landing on Runway 24 Right is C-FCPZ *"Empress of Los Angeles,"* a Boeing 737-217.

December 1985

In 1958, nine years after Pacific Southwest Airlines (PSA) inaugurated passenger service, Los Angeles was finally added to the small, intra-state route network. Douglas DC-4 aircraft were used to provide non-stop service to both San Francisco and San Diego. During late 1959, the airline took delivery of its first Lockheed Electra *"Prop-Jet"* for use on the Los Angeles-San Francisco route and allowed the little airline to compete directly with established carriers, Western and United Airlines. Los Angeles eventually became the hub of operations and when the McDonnell Douglas MD-80 was placed into service in November 1980, flights and passenger capacity increased at the airport. By 1985, the airline was flying over seventy-five daily flights from LAX and serving sixteen cities, yet the original Los Angeles-San Francisco *"California Corridor"* route continued to be most popular. Having just been pushed back from Terminal 1 for an early morning departure is N934PS, a McDonnell Douglas DC-9-81 (MD-81).

December 1985
In an effort to increase capacity on some of its popular trunk routes, Republic Airlines ordered six Boeing 757 airplanes, with the first aircraft being delivered on December 6, 1985. The first three 757s sold to Republic were originally destined for Indian Airlines, which cancelled their order thus allowing Republic an immediate purchase. The newly delivered planes were quickly put into the airline's winter schedule and placed on the *"Snow Bird"* routes, including flying from its Detroit hub to both Phoenix and Tampa. The narrow-body, twin-jet, was also scheduled on the longer, heavy capacity West Coast services, with flights from Detroit and Memphis to both Los Angeles and San Francisco. The airlines last Boeing 757 was delivered in June 1986, only four months before Northwest Orient Airlines would acquire Republic Airlines, and absorb the six 757s into its own fleet. Seen just weeks after having been delivered in its smart colors, N602RC, a Boeing 757-2S7, holds in position for takeoff on Runway 25 Left.

December 1985

During the energy crisis of the late 1970s, airlines were desperate to utilize the most efficient airplanes to keep ticket costs down for their passengers. After reviewing various options, Eastern Airlines agreed to a *"demonstration"* period of flying the new European airliner, the Airbus A-300. The first plane was delivered to the airline in August 1977, and started flying along the Eastern Seaboard. Pleased with the performance and operating costs, Eastern ordered twenty of the planes and became the first U.S. airline to put the A-300 into passenger service. The new Airbus *"Whisperliner"* was primarily used on the Miami-New York flights before being placed on transcontinental service and becoming popular on routes between Los Angeles and both Atlanta and Miami. Eastern became the largest operator of the Airbus A-300 in North America, eventually flying thirty-five of the type. Taxiing toward the departure end of Runway 24 Left during a soggy winter morning is N226EA, an Airbus A-300-B4-103.

January 1986

Another short-lived carrier to enter the popular California-Hawaii market was Air Hawaii, which started operations in the fall of 1985. Air Hawaii was started by the same owner of the previous airline, The Hawaii Express, and was again guaranteeing low fares and *"High Class"* on the popular Honolulu, Hawaii route. Using two leased Douglas DC-10s, the airline started flights from Los Angeles to Honolulu on November 22, 1985. A month later, flights were added from San Francisco to Honolulu, however, even during the busy winter season, the airline quickly ran into trouble. It was soon realized that competing with established carriers such as United, Western, and Continental, resulted in heavy financial losses in the first few months of operation. The airline continued to struggle and shut down only two months later, eventually filing for bankruptcy in February 1986. Displaying the simple, yet elegant, *"Bird of Paradise"* colors while taxiing toward the terminal after landing is N183AT, a Douglas DC-10-10.

January 1986
Pan American Airways was arguably one of the most recognized airlines to grace the global commercial aviation industry. Under the direction of the infamous Juan Trippe, Pan American started flying a mail contract in 1927, between Key West, Florida and Havana, Cuba. The airline continued to expand into the Caribbean, South America, and Pacific Rim, at which point, Los Angeles was added to the network in 1940, with flights to Honolulu. When the first Boeing 707 jet arrived at Pan Am in 1958, the airline was serving over forty cities on five continents. As new Boeing 747 jets arrived in 1970, Los Angeles was connected by Pan Am to the five international cities of Sydney, Tokyo, London, Caracas, and Guatemala City. With the acquisition of National Airlines in 1980, Pan Am's domestic network expanded, allowing the carrier to serve twelve cities from LAX, including four international destinations. Taxiing toward Runway 24 Left for a morning departure is N203PA *"Clipper New York,"* an Airbus A-300B4-203.

January 1986

Burlington Northern was traditionally known as a freight railroad company operating within the Pacific Northern regions of the United States. During 1985, the company ventured into the air freight market as Burlington Air Express and contracted with a variety of cargo airlines for space on their aircraft. In late 1985, with continued strong growth, Burlington purchased converted Douglas DC-8s, Boeing 707s, and Boeing 727s, then established its own air freight hub at Fort Wayne, Indiana. A route network was developed by the cargo airline to serve major U.S. cities specializing in overnight packages and bulk freight such as electronics and automotive parts. Los Angeles was considered a major freight market and was served by daily flights using the larger capacity Boeing 707s or Douglas DC-8s. Burlington Air Express would serve Los Angeles through the 1980s and into the 1990s. Parked at the south cargo ramp and awaiting its evening deliveries is N870BX *"Carl Taccini,"* a Douglas DC-8-63AF.

March 1986

Air California was eager to add Los Angeles to its timetable, one of the last major airports not served by the growing, regional airline. The carrier finally received approval in July 1980, and flights were started to both Fresno and Monterey. With a name change to AirCal and its *"foot in the door,"* the airline quickly expanded at Los Angeles and by 1983, had added flights to the cities of Oakland, Reno, San Jose, and San Francisco. Although facing fierce competition with established airlines, such as PSA, United, and Western on the lucrative San Francisco route, AirCal offered no less than ten flights a day to the *"Golden Gate"* city. AirCal became a major regional carrier at Los Angeles until its purchase by American Airlines in 1987. American acquired much coveted gate space and landing slots with the purchase and operated much of AirCal's established network until about 1990, when the planes and routes were sold off. Parked at the gate during an early spring morning is EI-ASH, a Boeing 737-248.

April 1986

Queensland and Northern Territory Aerial Services Ltd., better known as QANTAS, was established in November 1920, and started overseas service to Singapore in 1935. In 1947, the Australian Government assumed ownership of the airline and in 1958, started trans-Pacific service to San Francisco via Fiji and Honolulu using its new, Lockheed Super Constellation airplanes. Flights to Los Angeles didn't start until August 1980, when Boeing 747 service was introduced from Sydney, via Honolulu or Papeete. QANTAS was one of the few airlines that ordered Boeing's Special Performance, long-range 747. When the two 747SPs were delivered in 1981, they were used to inaugurate non-stop flights from Sydney to Los Angeles, which at that time, became the longest flight in the world. Both the Boeing 747 and 747SP services continued into LAX until the late 1980s, when they were replaced with the newer 747-400 series. Enroute to the International Terminal is VH-EBL *"City of Townsville,"* a Boeing 747-238B.

July 1986
Realizing a strong business opportunity, Royal West Airlines was formed to fly passengers from various West Coast cities to the popular Las Vegas, Nevada gambling market. The new airline ordered three, 91-passenger, British Aerospace BAe 146 airplanes, with the first airplane being delivered in June 1986. Scheduled flights started a few days later, from both Las Vegas and Reno, Nevada to Los Angeles, Burbank, and Ontario, California. Although the airline had five convenient daily departures from Los Angeles, it struggled with the competition in the market from both established carriers, Pacific Southwest Airlines (PSA) and America West Airlines. The airline eventually focused more of its business efforts on tour groups, and even started a non-stop service between Los Angeles and Vail-Eagle, Colorado, for the winter ski season. Despite various marketing strategies, the airline filed for bankruptcy in February 1987. Awaiting taxi clearance from ground control is N801RW, a British Aerospace BAe 146-100.

September 1986
Malaysian Airline System or MAS became the government owned airline of Malaysia in 1971, when the existing Malaysian-Singapore Airlines (MSA) was dissolved. Early services focused on a modest domestic and regional route structure from its home country using both the Fokker F-27 and Boeing 737. International services were started in 1973, to Hong Kong and Indonesia and within two years had extended flights to both Australia and Japan, using the Boeing 707. Seeking to extend further across the globe, MAS placed an order for the Boeing 747, having the first delivered in 1982, for service to Europe. Authority was granted in 1986, to serve the United States and Los Angeles would be the first city to see service by the airline. A twice weekly, trans-Pacific flight routed Kuala Lumpur-Tokyo-Los Angeles was flown using the long-range Boeing 747. Seen turning onto Runway 24 Left for an afternoon departure and proudly displaying the introduction of service to Los Angeles is 9M-MHK, a Boeing 747-3H6 Combi.

October 1986
Another 1980s Airbus operator was Continental Airlines, which had originally considered purchasing the Airbus A-300 airliner in 1977, when the manufacturer was promoting North American sales, yet never did order the aircraft. Almost a decade later, Continental re-evaluated the European airliner as an aircraft that could fly medium range or transcontinental routings with economical per seat-mile costs. In April 1986, Continental initially purchased six of the planes from Airbus, which had a capacity of 272-passengers, in a two-class configuration. The A-300 was used on trunk routes such as, Denver-Seattle, Houston-Miami, and Newark-Orlando. Los Angeles was one of the first cities to be served by the plane, which was used on flights to both Denver and Houston. Continental would eventually operate eighteen of the successful European airliners, until high maintenance and lease costs resulted in their removal from service in 1995. Holding short of Runway 25 Right is N972C, an Airbus A-300B4-203.

January 1987
The national airline of Germany was originally established with the merger of two, smaller carriers into Deutsche Luft Hansa, to provide passenger services in 1926. Until the end of the World War II, passenger air service in Germany effectively came to a halt. After the war, it took many years to reorganize a national airline and in 1954, Luftag was formed to provide passenger services. A year later, with continued growth, the name was changed to Lufthansa. The airline quickly expanded and purchased the Boeing 707 *"Intercontinental Jet"* for international services. In 1969, flights were started to Los Angeles, as an extension of its popular Frankfurt-Paris-Montréal route, using the Boeing 707. Lufthansa was the first airline outside the United States to order the Boeing 747, with the first plane being delivered in 1970, and being placed on long-haul routes to North America and the Far East. Starting to flare for landing, after a non-stop flight from Frankfurt is D-ABYJ *"Hessen,"* a Boeing 747-230B Combi.

March 1987
Consolidated Freightways was a major land based freight forwarder founded in Portland, Oregon in 1929. The company specialized in Less-than-Truckload freight and built up a fleet of trucks to meet customer's demands. During 1966, Consolidated Freightways formed a subsidiary, known as CF Air Freight, for the growing need of air cargo service and leased cargo space on various airlines. The lease agreement worked for many years, but new customers and binding schedules finally required CF to operate its own aircraft. In early 1987, CF leased three Boeing 727s and two Boeing 707s from Southern Air Transport, with all five aircraft painted in the familiar CF colors. The 707s were used on the busier routes from the carrier's Indianapolis base including flights to Los Angeles, itself being a major freight market. During 1989, CF purchased Emery Worldwide to become one of the world's largest freight forwarders. Awaiting another load of freight at the south cargo ramp is N526SJ, a Boeing 707-338C.

June 1987

SkyWest Airlines started operations in 1972, flying a route from its home base of St. George, Utah, to Salt Lake City. After acquiring its first Metro turboprop in 1979, the small airline expanded from Utah to serve the neighboring cities of Phoenix and Las Vegas. By 1984, the airline was flying to eighteen cities in seven Western states and in a move to increase its California market presence, purchased the Palm Springs based commuter airline, Sun Aire. Within a year, SkyWest was flying twenty-six Metroliners and signed an agreement with Western Airlines to become that carriers commuter carrier. After Delta Airlines purchased Western Airlines in 1987, SkyWest became a *"Delta Connection"* carrier and had become the largest *"airline"* operating from LAX with over one-hundred daily flights serving fourteen regional cities including Palmdale, Santa Maria, Inyokern, and San Diego. Seen getting ready to depart the Delta commuter ramp is N186SW, an Embraer EMB-120RT Brasilia.

March 1987

The Civil Aviation Administration of China, or CAAC, was formed in 1949, by the Chinese government to control commercial aviation in the newly formed Peoples Republic of China. An extensive network of domestic routes was established over the next decade and with the addition of Boeing 707 aircraft in 1973, international services were started to Europe, the Middle East, and Japan. A Boeing 747 Special Performance aircraft was delivered to the airline in 1980, and this allowed for inauguration of non-stop, trans-Pacific service to San Francisco from Shanghai. Los Angeles was added to the CAAC network in 1982, as a final stop to becoming the airline's popular, Beijing-Shanghai-San Francisco-Los Angeles route. In 1987, the Chinese government sought to reorganize the airline and CAAC was dissolved to become Air China and seven separate domestic carriers within the country of China. Making its way along Taxiway Uniform toward the departure end of Runway 24 Left is N1304E, a Boeing 747SP-J6.

August 1987

The national airline of Japan was formed by private interests in 1951, and started a modest, domestic network with Martin 202 aircraft. International passenger services started in 1954, with flights to San Francisco using a Douglas DC-6B. Recognizing the potential for an all freight, trans-Pacific service, Japan Airlines formed the Cargo Division of the airline in 1959, and started cargo flights to San Francisco from Tokyo, using a Douglas DC-4 freighter. A year later, jet cargo service was started using a mixed configuration Douglas DC-8, and in 1969, the airline took delivery of its first pure freighter, a Douglas DC-8-F *"Jet Trader."* Combination passenger/cargo flights started into Los Angeles in 1969, followed by pure cargo flights in the early 1970s. JAL Cargo received its first Boeing 747 Freighter in 1974, for use on routes to North America and Europe. LAX received the *"Jumbo"* freighter in the early 1980s, for non-stop cargo flights to Japan. Parked at the JAL Cargo ramp is JA8151, a Boeing 747-246F.

August 1987

Flying the mail was where commercial aviation truly evolved, as airlines were initially formed to fly government mail contracts. The first mail contracts issued in 1918, took priority and flights and routes were developed based upon where the mail needed to go. Passengers, if carried, were considered secondary. As the airline industry developed, passenger operations became the primary focus and the bulk of mail transport reverted back to land based methods, such as truck or train. During the late 1970s, the post office saw new air cargo carriers begin to add an element of competition to express package service. In 1987, the US Postal Service opened an express mail hub at Terre Haute, Indiana, and contracted Evergreen International Airlines to fly postal specific flights to numerous cities, including Los Angeles. A variety of Douglas DC-8s and Boeing 727s were painted with the familiar post office logo and colors for this service. On its daily layover at the south cargo ramp is N728EV, a Boeing 727-78.

February 1988

All Nippon Airways, better known as ANA, started operations in 1958, and was to become Japan's second largest airline. Initially focusing its efforts on passenger services between Japan's larger cities, ANA utilized a variety of aircraft in the early years such as the Douglas DC-3, Convair 440, and the Fokker F-27 turboprop. Over the next twenty years, ANA had an unprecedented amount of growth due to strong population and economic expansion in Japan. The airline entered the jet-age in 1964, using the Boeing 727, from a Tokyo hub to various *"Beam Lines"* throughout Japan. With passenger numbers continuing to increase the airline placed into service the Lockheed L-1011 and Boeing 747 during the mid-1970s. Seeking to expand beyond its *"domestic"* status, ANA was granted permission to start flights into the United States in 1986. Services from Tokyo to Los Angeles were started in July 1986, followed by flights to Washington D.C. Starting its takeoff rotation on Runway 24 Left is JA8181, a Boeing 747-281B.

February 1988

American Airlines in an effort to bring passengers from smaller, regional locations into its hub airports created American Eagle in 1984, as its own commuter carrier. The first airline to establish flights under the American Eagle banner was commuter Metro Airlines based at Dallas-Ft. Worth. Pleased with the results, American Airlines sought other partners and looked to Wings West Airlines to provide *"Eagle"* flights to its rather large operations at Los Angeles. In June 1986, Wings West became an American Eagle affiliate feeding passengers to American Airlines at both Los Angeles and San Francisco airports. During 1987, American Airlines purchased Wings West outright and continued to operate American Eagle flights along the West Coast. By 1988, over seventy daily flights were being flown from LAX to thirteen cities including Bakersfield, Fresno, Lake Tahoe, and San Diego. Parked at the Terminal 4 commuter ramp during a passing rain storm is N362AE, a Fairchild Swearingen SA-227AC Metro III.

March 1988

UTA-Union de Transports Aeriens, was formed in 1963, by the merger of two independent French airlines, Union Aeromaritime de Transports (UAT) and Transports Aeriens Intercontinentaux (TAI). The new airline became the second largest in France and focused its efforts on overseas destinations including routes to Africa, Asia, and the Pacific. TAI was the original airline starting service into Los Angeles in 1960, with flights from Papeete, Tahiti via Honolulu using Douglas DC-7C aircraft. Later that year, with the delivery of its first Douglas DC-8, TAI started non-stop service to Los Angeles from Tahiti, becoming one of the longest, non-stop flights in the world at the time. During 1973, UTA took delivery of its first Douglas DC-10, which became the equipment of choice on the popular trans-Pacific route during the decade of the 1980s. Having just been pushed out from the International Terminal is F-BTDE, a Douglas DC-10-30, which also wears the titles of Aeromaritime, a charter company once owned by UTA.

April 1988
Alaska Airlines can trace its roots back to 1934, and the development of McGee Airways which started service between Anchorage and Bristol Bay, Alaska using a three-seat Stinson airplane. Through various mergers and acquisitions of smaller air carriers, Alaska Airlines was formed in 1944. Although early operations focused on flights within Alaska, the airline extended service to the *"Lower 48"* in 1951, using a Douglas DC-4 on flights to Seattle from Fairbanks. After airline deregulation, Alaska sought to expand services and started flights into San Francisco, California in 1979. Flights were eventually extended further south and Los Angeles was added to the route map with Boeing 727 service to Seattle in June 1985. By the end of the 1980s, Alaska Airlines had added Portland, Oregon, San Diego and Los Cabos, Mexico as additional destinations from Los Angeles. Wearing the famous *"Smiling Eskimo"* and taking Runway 25 Left for a mid-morning departure is N304AS, a Boeing 727-227.

June 1988

The national airline of Yugoslavia, Jugoslovenski Aerotransport or JAT, was formed in 1947, during the post-World War II recovery. The new, government owned airline started both domestic and regional Eastern European routes before having to cancel most flights a few years later due to political turmoil. Yugoslavia aligned with the West and reestablished the airline in 1950. Operations started to North America in 1970 using the Boeing 707, followed by the purchase of two Douglas DC-10s which allowed the airline to expand its reach globally. During the mid-1980s, JAT went through a period of rapid growth eventually serving eighty destinations on five continents. Los Angeles was added in 1987, as an extension of its Chicago-Zagreb service using the Douglas DC-10. The twice weekly service to Los Angeles lasted only a few years however due to eventual civil unrest in Yugoslavia. Taking Runway 24 Left for an evening departure is OO-SLA, a Douglas DC-10-30CF leased out from SABENA Belgium.

October 1988
Another California airline that would acquire the ultra-quiet, British made regional jet, was commuter WestAir Airlines. In 1986, WestAir officially became a United Express carrier and would operate in full United Airlines colors. WestAir started operations in 1972 as a small, regional commuter based in Chico, California, and provided flights to various destinations in Northern California. The airline became a United Express partner in 1986, and started service into Los Angeles in 1987. The airline ordered six British Aerospace BAe 146 aircraft in July 1988, to provide feeder services for the United Airlines hubs at both Los Angeles and San Francisco, where United's regular airline fleet was uneconomical on the longer, thinner regional routes. From Los Angeles, the ninety-passenger planes flew regular service to both Fresno and Monterey, California, as well as to Reno, Nevada. Seen completing final checks before pushing back from Terminal 7 for a mid-day flight is N295UE, a British Aerospace BAe 146-200.

November 1988

When Allegheny Airlines changed its name to USAir in 1979, the new airline was truly trying to be a *"U.S."* carrier and sought expansion toward the lucrative West Coast market. In February 1983, USAir started non-stop service from Pittsburgh to both Los Angeles and San Francisco using the Boeing 727 on the cross-country flights. Along with Southwest Airlines, USAir was the launch customer of the second generation, Boeing 737-300 series, and was the first airline to take delivery in November 1984. The new plane had transcontinental range and allowed USAir to increase capacity from Los Angeles to Pittsburgh and add flights to Indianapolis. By 1987, the airline had also added flights from Los Angeles to San Diego, San Francisco, and Phoenix using both the Boeing 727 and 737. USAir would gain a huge increase in presence at LAX with the purchase of PSA in 1986, followed by the purchase of Piedmont Airlines a year later. Taxiing inbound, toward its gate at Terminal 1 is N514AU, a Boeing 737-3B7.

November 1988
Formed in North Carolina during 1948, Piedmont grew to become a respected international airline with hundreds of flights a day. Piedmont Airlines remained regional in nature, focusing its flight activity east of the Rocky Mountains until the early 1980s. With numerous airlines based along the Eastern Seaboard starting service to the West, Piedmont was no exception. In April 1984, transcontinental service was started to Los Angeles, from its base of Charlotte and hub of Dayton, using Boeing 727s. Due to increased demand and sector length on certain domestic routes as well as approval of service to London, England, Piedmont ordered six Boeing 767-200 Extended Range aircraft. Although, mainly used on the trans-Atlantic flights to Europe, the new wide-body airplane was also placed on the popular, transcontinental routes to both Los Angeles and San Francisco. Taxiing up to the gate at Terminal 1 is N614P *"City of Los Angeles,"* a Boeing 767-212ER, appropriately named for its important destination.

December 1988

Mexico has a strong connection with the Los Angeles region and the two major Mexican airlines that served the airport were evidence of this fact. Considered the fourth oldest airline in the world when founded as Compañía Mexicana de Transportación Aérea in 1921, Mexicana was also the first international airline to start service into Los Angeles in April 1934, using a Lockheed L-10 Electra, on a multi-stop flight to Mexico City. Mexicana followed this milestone in 1960, by introducing non-stop jet service from Mexico City, using the luxurious de Havilland Comet. A few years later in 1962, Aeronavis de Mexico started flights into Los Angeles, later becoming Aeromexico. By 1988, both airlines considered LAX an international gateway airport and together were serving eight destinations in Mexico, including the popular Mexico City and Guadalajara flights. Having just been pushed back for a flight is XA-DEM *"La Paz BC,"* a Douglas DC-9-32, with Mexicana's XA-MXG *"Monterrey,"* a Boeing 727-2A1, parked at the gate.

July 1989
When Aero California started international jet flights in 1989, the airline had been in business for almost thirty years serving the State of Baja California, Mexico. The airline was founded in 1960, to provide charter service between small communities within the rugged Baja Peninsula. Many of the flights used Cessna 402, Douglas DC-3, and Convair 340 equipment on a variety of routes to small fishing villages from a base in La Paz, Mexico. In June 1982, the airline purchased a Douglas DC-9 to provide scheduled jet service to mainland Mexico on a Tijuana-Los Mochis-Guadalajara route. During 1989, the airline saw the opportunity to start flights from Baja California into the United States, and applied for service which was quickly approved. In June 1989, using an additional leased Douglas DC-9, flights were started into Los Angeles with service to the fishing/resort town of Loreto, located on the Sea of Cortez. Taxiing away from the International Terminal for a trans-border flight is XA-LMM, a Douglas DC-9-14.

August 1989

Air BC was formed in 1980, with the merger of five, smaller passenger airlines, flying various routes along the Pacific Coast in British Columbia, Canada. The de Havilland DHC-6 Twin Otter was the workhorse of the early fleet, suited best for the rugged conditions encountered. Within a few years, the airline added the de Havilland DHC-7 *"Dash 7"* turboprop from its Vancouver base. During 1987, Air Canada purchased a majority of Air BC's shares and incorporated flights into the Air Canada Connector schedule. Wanting to increase capacity and range on longer routes, the airline acquired five British Aerospace BAe 146 jets in May 1988, using the new planes on flights from Vancouver to Price Rupert, Kitimat, and Whitehorse. During the summer tourist season in 1989, the airline started charter and tour group flights to San Francisco and Los Angeles, California, and Reno, Nevada, lasting through September of that year. Enroute to Terminal 2 after having landed is C-FBAV, a British Aerospace BAe 146-200.

August 1989

Los Angeles's hometown commuter airline Air LA, started service in 1982, from Burbank Airport as a scheduled air tour operator using Cessna 402 and Piper Navajo equipment. Tour packages focused on scenic flights to the Grand Canyon, with extensions to Las Vegas, Nevada, as needed. In 1986, additional cities including Ontario, California, and Bullhead City, Arizona, were added to establish more of a *"commuter"* network. In 1988, the airline moved its operations to Los Angeles International Airport and located its facilities south of the main terminals, at the Imperial Terminal, thereby allowing less congestion and delay for its passengers. Two BAe Jetstream turboprops were leased in December 1988, to carry passengers on an enhanced route network, including airports that had not been served by passenger airlines in years, such as Blythe and Bermuda Dunes-Palm Desert. Heading toward Runway 25 Left for a mid-day departure is N332QC *"Desert Starship,"* a British Aerospace BAe Jetstream 3201.

November 1989

One of the first airlines to start passenger service into Los Angeles, was United Airlines predecessor, Pacific Air Transport, which started a multi-stop service between Seattle and Los Angeles in 1926. A series of mergers created United Airlines in 1931, and within a few years, United had added non-stop flights from Los Angeles to San Diego and San Francisco, using the Boeing 247 airplane. In September 1959, United entered the jet age by placing its first Douglas DC-8 in service and commencing non-stop flights from Los Angeles to New York a month later in October. The airline was the launch customer for the medium range Boeing 767, placing an order for thirty aircraft in 1978, and receiving its first in 1982. The wide-body Boeings were immediately placed on high capacity routes connecting Los Angeles with Denver, Chicago, and San Francisco. Having just touched down on Runway 7 Right during a late fall Santa Ana wind event is N614UA, a Boeing 767-222, in the well-recognized Saul Bass colors.

November 1989
Midway Airlines, which was initially formed in October 1976, became the first new airline to begin operations following the Airline Deregulation Act of 1978. Based at Chicago's Midway airport, the airline started flights in November 1979, operating the Douglas DC-9 airplane to numerous cities, mainly within the eastern region of the United States. During 1984, the airline acquired many of the routes and aircraft of the former Air Florida and expanded into the Southeast. Seeking to extend its routes further west, Midway ordered the McDonnell Douglas MD-87, with a longer range and more fuel-efficient operations. New westbound flights commenced on May 1, 1989, when non-stop service to Los Angeles was started from Chicago's Midway Airport. The route proved popular with passengers, as an alternative airport in the Chicago area, until the airline filed for bankruptcy in 1991. Caught touching down on Runway 7 Right after a mid-day flight is N802ML, a McDonnell Douglas MD-87.

November 1989

In 1987, Kirk Kerkorian, a multi-millionaire businessman, established MGM Grand Air to provide luxury airline flights to clientele expecting the best in amenities and service. Three Boeing 727-100 airplanes were purchased and heavily modified to provide *"Grand Class"* service for thirty-four passengers. Each airplane was fitted with sleeper seats, fax machines, air-phones, and laptop outlets, all of which were uncommon on the mainline carriers at the time. Based at Los Angeles, scheduled flights between Los Angeles-Las Vegas, Las Vegas-New York, and New York-Los Angeles, completed a *"Golden Triangle"* of service, which was promoted to customers. The airline soon became popular with various movie, sports, and music stars, which chartered the aircraft on a regular basis. MGM Grand Air eventually discontinued scheduled service in 1992, in lieu of charter flights. Taxiing outbound from the Imperial Terminal to the runway on a foggy autumn morning is N503MG, a Boeing 727-191.

November 1989

Mexicana Airlines, along with competitor Aeromexico, were the only two airlines to place orders for the special Douglas DC-10, series -15 model. The -15 was considered the *"Hot and High"* version, with increased thrust engines, necessary for optimum takeoff performance from the Mexico City airport, which is at an elevation of 7,300 feet and having typical summer temperatures above 80°F. Mexicana ordered five of the 315-passenger, series -15 aircraft, the first being delivered in June 1981. The Douglas DC-10 *"wide-bodies,"* were a first for Mexico and immediately placed in service on the airline's major trunk routes, including one of its most important; the Los Angeles-Mexico City international routing. Additional flights from Los Angeles using the high capacity DC-10 were on non-stop services to Guadalajara and during the winter tourist season, to the seaside resort of Puerto Vallarta. Having just touched down on Runway 25 Left and in full reverse thrust is N10045 *"Maya,"* a Douglas DC-10-15.

February 1990

During the late 1980s, a number of charter companies were formed in Mexico to provide service to that country's numerous seaside resorts and cities. Aerocancun was founded in 1989, by a group of Mexican investors and Oasis International, a hotel owner. As the airline's name suggests, the airline was based at the tourist destination of Cancun, located on the Gulf of Mexico. Early plans were to provide flights to Europe, yet the airline focused its initial efforts on the United States market and leased two McDonnell Douglas MD-83 aircraft. Just in time for the winter tourist season, flights started in November 1989, to various destinations in the United States, including Baltimore, New York, Chicago, and Memphis. Charter flights from Los Angeles to Cancun started on December 15, 1989. Due to devaluation of the Mexican Peso and decreasing tourism, the airline had to file for bankruptcy in 1996. Having just been pushed back from the International Terminal is XA-RPH, a McDonnell Douglas MD-83.

February 1990

Ecuatoriana was the national flag carrier of the South American country of Ecuador. Originally started by private investors in 1957, full control by the government didn't take place until 1974, which by then, the airline was flying to Miami, Bogotá, Panama City, and Mexico City, with a fleet of two Boeing 720s and Lockheed Electras. With control by the government, Ecuatoriana's daily operations became the responsibility of the Ecuadorian Air Force, which provided the airline an additional four Boeing 707s for expansion of international services. Los Angeles was added to the schedule in early 1977, with flights to both Mexico City and Guayaquil, Ecuador. With the addition of Douglas DC-10 equipment in 1983, the airline was able to open new routes to Canada and Europe. The Boeing 707s would be used to provide services through the 1980s, being one of the last mainline airlines to do so. Parked at the west holding area and waiting for an evening turn-around is HC-BFC *"Chimborazo,"* a Boeing 707-321B.

Future Departed Wings books in development

Departed Wings-Southern California
Burbank (BUR)-Long Beach (LGB)-Ontario (ONT)-Orange County (SNA)-San Diego (SAN)

Departed Wings-Northern California
Monterey (MRY)-San Francisco (SFO)-San Jose (SJC)

Visit us at www.departedwings.com for regular updates